My etchings, books and puzzles are available year round at pm gallery, 726 N. High St. in the Short North. Coming up: a solo show of new etchings and drawings at pm October 3-31. Original drawings from The History of the Universe Vol. II will be on view at the Worthington Library during the month of December.

THE HISTORY OF THE UNIVERSE

VOL. I

SUSAN STURGILL

Susan Sturgill 6/8/92

The Laughing Academy Press
P.O. Box 02061 • Columbus, Ohio 43202

In grateful acknowledgement of all the people who helped me think up jokes. You know who you are. I'll always love you. The check is in the mail.

ISBN 0-9626108-0-1

This book was manufactured in the U.S.A. for The Laughing Academy Press in a first edition of 2500 copies, April 1, 1988. Second printing of 1000 copies April 1, 1992 by Worzalla Publishing Co., Stevens Point, Wisconsin.

"…of making many books there is no end…"
—Ecclesiastes 11:12

For Uncle Bob

The Creator is no square-thumbed
Huguenot scrambling ass-over-wattle along the
trade routes to collect the rent money. God is
not an economist. God is, in fact, jaunty.

—Alexander Theroux
Three Wogs

"As I get it," Jack said, "Your God is two gentlemen and a bird."

—William Kennedy
Legs

Chapter 1: Creation

ON THE FOURTH DAY HE SET LIGHTS IN THE FIRMAMENT OF HEAVEN

ON THE FIFTH MORNING GOD COOKED UP SOME PRIMORDIAL SOUP

ON THE SIXTH NIGHT GOD CREATED WOMEN THAT MORNING. WINE AND SONG (HE'D ALREADY MADE

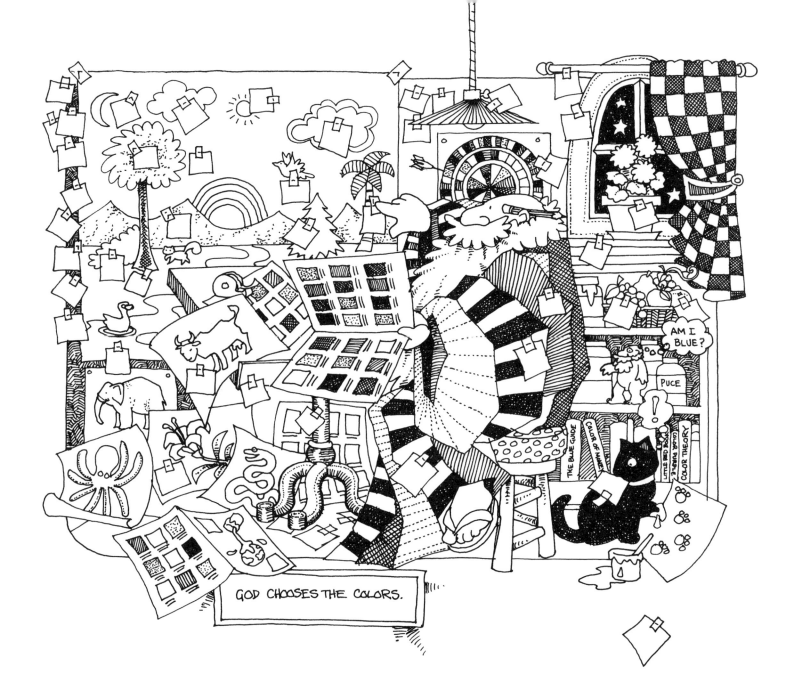

Chapter 2: Commandments

THE TWELFTH COMMANDMENT

EVE SURRENDERS TO TEMPTATION...

....GOD HANDS DOWN THE THIRTEENTH COMMANDMENT.

Chapter 3: Life in Heaven

GOD'S ONLY NEPHEW

GOD AT THE BEACH

THE GREAT FLOOD

SATURDAY NIGHT OF THE GODS

GOD'S IN HIS HOT TUB, ALL'S RIGHT WITH THE WORLD...

TO THE THERMAL FEATURES

Chapter 4: The End

Chapter 5: Appendices

GOD – FATHER. BABY JESUS – SON. PARAKEET – PARACLETE (GET IT?), A WORD FROM THE GREEK MEANING "HOLY SPIRIT." I ADMIT I HAVE NOT READ THIS IN A BOOK BUT I HEARD IT IN A SERMON IN CHURCH SO IT MUST BE RIGHT. CAT — THERE IS NO DOCUMENTATION FOR THIS. I MADE IT UP.

APPENDIX III:

GOD'S ONLY DAUGHTERS: AGNES AND GLORIA DEI

Susan Sturgill grew up in Cincinnati, Ohio where she was an attentive Sunday school student. Now a freelance illustrator in Columbus, her work has appeared in many regional publications, on jigsaw puzzles and in textbooks. She founded The Laughing Academy Press (Ego adsum quod insana non stulta) to serve her own vanity in publishing *The History of the Universe Vol. I* in 1988. *Only Two (Seems Like More)*, a book about her cats, followed in 1990 and *The History of the Universe Vol. II* in 1992. Earlier books of her own material not self-published are *The Frog Prince* (New Rivers Press, NY, 1977) and *Animal Fair* (Cricket Publications, Toledo OH, 1983).